Designed for Purpose

A Devotional

By Vann Mizzelle Lassiter

Designed for Purpose
By Vann Mizzelle Lassiter

ISBN-13: 978-0692598924
ISBN-10: 0692598928

Published by Vann Mizzelle Lassiter

Scripture quotations marked (NIV) are taken from the Holy Bible, New International Version®, NIV®. Copyright © 1973, 1978, 1984, 2011 by Biblica, Inc.™ Used by permission of Zondervan. All rights reserved worldwide. www.zondervan.com The "NIV" and "New International Version" are trademarks registered in the United States Patent and Trademark Office by Biblica, Inc.™

Scripture quotations marked (KJV) are taken from **The Holy Bible, King James Version** by public domain.

Author email: vannlassiter@gmail.com

Facebook page:
www.facebook.com/designedforpurpose7

Cover design by JudyVandiver.com

Printed in the United States of America
First Edition 2016

DEDICATION

To my family who loved me, friends who supported me, teachers who encouraged me, and students who challenged me.

Every great dream begins with a dreamer. Always remember, you have within you the strength, the patience, and the passion to reach for the stars to change the world.

~ Harriet Tubman[i]

Vann Mizzelle Lassiter

CONTENTS

PREFACE

This book was birthed with the mission to encourage and inspire. The age-old question, *"What is my purpose?"* has left many pondering their life's goals, dreams, desires, and reasons for living and being. Through personal experiences and life lessons learned from many of the greats, I have discovered the importance of being true to myself, confident in my God-given gifts and abilities, and understanding the impact change—both expected and unexpected—has in my life. Each change has led and guided me into purpose—on purpose.

In the midst of life's journeys of ups and downs, as we seek to obtain our goals and dreams, we may not always recognize the answers to the questions, Why? Why me? Why now? Why this way? Why am I alive? It is important to remember that everything that happens (or doesn't happen) in life has a purpose. It's all ordained. Every situation or circumstance we experience, each person or group we encounter, any job held or lost, any strength or weakness we possess, the body in which our soul resides, and our talents and gifts make us who we are. To God, nothing in our life is a surprise. We are designed on purpose, by purpose.

"The purpose of life is to live it, to taste experience to the utmost, to reach out eagerly and without fear for newer and richer experiences."

~ Eleanor Roosevelt[ii]

CHAPTER 1

Born Purposed

People spend many hours pondering and trying to understand their purpose, which often only leads to even more questions. In order to understand our purpose, it is essential that we understand its meaning.

The word *purpose*, by definition, can be used as either a noun or a verb. According to *Merriam-Webster*, in the noun form, *purpose* is the reason for which something is done or created, or for which something exists. The verb form of this word means to have as one's intention or objective.[iii] Based on these definitions and understanding, one can conclude that we live or exist (life) with meaning and an assignment to accomplish (purpose).

I am not implying that life's journey will be easy or free of challenges. Be assured that no matter what, we have a purpose, a destiny. Understanding the definition, understanding Who created us, Who purposed us, and Who designed us sheds a bright light on *why* and *for what*. It's incredibly amazing to think that the Creator of all things, the One named above all, and the Giver of life, purpose, and mission created us on purpose and for a purpose. Who? Our Lord and Savior Jesus Christ.

Genesis 1:27-28 in the King James Version tells us, "So God created man in his own image, in the image of God created he him: male and female created he them. And God blessed them, and God said unto them, be fruitful, and multiply, and replenish the earth, and subdue it: and have dominion over the fish of the sea, and over the fowl of the air, and over every living thing that moveth upon the earth." Here, we can see God's purposeful crafting of mankind and the assigning of a mission. This hasn't changed. Today, we still have a purpose and destiny.

How do we know our purpose? In knowing our passion, we can locate our purpose. Our gifts and talents are the roots of our purpose. God doesn't purpose us for something that He hasn't (or won't eventually) prepare us to do or accomplish with excellence and success. Everything we need to reach our destiny is inside us awaiting our willingness to follow it, obey, and lead under the guidance of the Lord.

Just as the flowers were purposed to release oxygen for humans to breathe and take in carbon dioxide to live and grow, we are designed to release that carbon dioxide and take in oxygen. Walking in our purpose is fruitful, positive, and life-giving. Walking in a purpose not assigned us can be stressful, undesirable, and sometimes dangerous. Do you know someone with the God-given ability to sing and someone else who does not have the gift but thinks he does? If not, think about some of the contestants on shows such as *American Idol, The*

Voice, or *Sunday's Best.* The tune from the individual who can't sing stresses our ears, as the sound is undesirable and our ability to enjoy the song is lost. On the other hand, the melody from the individual who has the ability to sing soothes our soul, and their talent welcomes us to listen and want more. When we do what we're equipped and commissioned to do, watch the blessings, favor, and success flow.

I am reminded of one of the greatest baseball players of all time, Babe Ruth. Born George Herman Ruth, Jr. in 1895, Ruth was sent to an orphanage at the age of seven. Ruth's parents, who owned a tavern, placed him in St. Mary's Industrial School for Boys. It was at this orphanage that a man named Brother Matthias taught young George how to play baseball. Many know Babe Ruth for his home run record (714 during his career), but along with all those home runs came a pretty hefty number of strikeouts. Ruth had a total of 1330. In fact, it's stated that for decades, he held the record for most baseball strikes. When asked about them, he would say, "Every strike brings me closer to the next home run." Ruth developed a passion for baseball and discovered his purpose in the process. Defeat along the way didn't keep him from doing what he was talented at—playing baseball. And through his struggles in life, he discovered his purpose—to be an example of encouragement to others.[iv]

This illustration serves as a reminder that God doesn't give life to someone without giving him or her a divine destiny. The beginning of our journey may be rocky or unsettling, and we may face obstacles along the way, but if we stand strong in faith, believing in God and remembering that we are all designed for a purpose, we shall accomplish that which God has ordained. There is power in the platform we've been given. Exploring our passions reveals our purpose.

PURPOSEFUL REFLECTIONS

Although circumstances may not be ideal, such as in the case of Babe Ruth being sent to an orphanage and striking out 1330 times, God's purpose always prevails. Purpose can't be stopped. In spite of his hardships, Babe Ruth became a world-renowned baseball player, one who inspired others. He, for a time, held the world record for most home runs.

The same can be true for us. We should walk with our heads high, knowing we are important and we are needed. No one else can do what we are individually purposed to do, the way we are purposed to do it. Stand in and on purpose!

"In their hearts humans plan their course, but the Lord establishes their steps." (Proverbs 16:9, NIV).

"Being confident of this very thing, that he which hath begun a good work in you will perform it until the day of Jesus Christ." (Philippians 1:6, KJV).

"In all thy ways acknowledge him, and he shall direct thy paths." (Proverbs 3:6, KJV).

"Who I am is God's gift to me, but what I do with those gifts – how I use them for life—my life—is my gift to God." Reverend Jerry W. Beaver[v]

The key is to focus on God's plan for *our lives.* We benefit greatly when we resist the temptation to compare ourselves or situations to someone else's. Enjoy the gifts and talents within instead of lusting after those of others. Remember that we are not running their race. We don't know what that other person had to go through to obtain what he has. We must run *our* race.

From the outside looking in, we acknowledge Babe Ruth for his greatness as a baseball player and his world record of home runs, but we did not have to live the journey that led to his greatness. Even after reading and learning of his hardships, the emotions, pain, sadness, joy, or excitement he felt on a personal level, we'll never fully understand it. We can, however, understand our own journey and do what God has purposed us to do.

It's important for us to be ourselves. You've probably noticed that when we do what we are not wired to do it drains us—physically or emotionally. But when we do what we are purposed to do, it invigorates us, and this is where we should focus our energy.

"For we are God's handiwork, created in Christ Jesus to do good works, which God prepared in advance for us to do." (Ephesians 2:10, NIV).

"For everything God created is good, and nothing is to be rejected if it is received with thanksgiving." (1 Timothy 4:4, NIV).

"Do not conform to the pattern of this world, but be transformed by the renewing of your mind. Then you will be able to test and approve what God's will

is – his good, pleasing and perfect will." (Romans 12:2, NIV).

When reaching for our purpose, we should surround ourselves with people who will build us up. Learn from those in our field. Improve our craft. Babe Ruth learned from Brother Matthis. Who taught or is teaching you? We all need support. Find those key individuals who are positive, uplifting, and encouraging.

"And do not forget to do good and to share with others, for with such sacrifices God is pleased." (Hebrews 13:16, NIV).

". . . not looking to your own interests but each of you to the interests of the others." (Philippians 2:4, NIV).

"If you want to go fast, go alone. If you want to go far, go together." (African Proverb).[vi]

Vann Mizzelle Lassiter

"You can have anything you want if you want it badly enough. You can be anything you want to be, do anything you set out to accomplish if you hold to that desire with singleness of purpose."

~Abraham Lincoln[vii]

Vann Mizzelle Lassiter

CHAPTER 2

No Accidents in Purpose

It was the day after my 20th birthday. I was heading home from college in hopes of celebrating with my family when life changed. On May 1, 2005, I packed my 1984 navy blue, 300 diesel Mercedes Benz, a gift from my grandfather, and started the two-and-a-half-hour drive to my small hometown. As I drove down the road, it began to rain . . . and rain . . . and rain. What started as a light drizzle turned into a downpour. The more it rained, the slower I drove and the faster my windshield wipers seemed to work. Being the cautious person that I am, I was driving under the speed limit, enjoying one of my favorite songs, "I Need You Now" by Smokie Norful. It was just my music, the road, and me.

About an hour into my trip, the steering wheel began to shake, and my tires wobbled. Before I knew it, my car hydroplaned and went into a spin. I turned the wheel in the correct direction, just as they'd taught in driver's education, and held on tight. The car spun a total of three times: the first into the second lane of traffic on my side of the road, the second into the opposite side, and the third back to my side before resting upon the embankment. Though this ordeal happened in a matter of minutes, it felt like a lifetime as every emotion possible flooded my mind—fear, worry, sadness, guilt, disappointment, shock, nervousness, and most of all, panic. As I sat behind the wheel of my automobile, still gripping it for dear life, I realized how *lucky* I had been to not hit any other cars. It seemed as if every single vehicle on the highway disappeared just long enough for my car to sweep across and back.

As I mentally relived the moment, I remember spinning, the song playing, me singing, and the moment the artist sang the words of the song that said, "Not a second or another minute . . . Not an hour of another day . . . But at this moment with my arms outstretched . . . I need you to make a way as you have done so many times before." The lyrics continued, reaching the heart of the song, "Not an hour of another day but, Lord . . . I need you right away."[viii] It was as if this song was aligned to every move, slide, and slip of my car during the accident. I had sung this song through the entire ordeal, my voice growing louder and louder as my panic grew. The song became my cry to God for help. My car landed in the ditch, facing in the right direction as if God heard every word I sang and prayed while I held onto that wheel. I realized at that moment, it wasn't *luck* but God's mercy that kept me safe.

I stepped out of the car and climbed to the top of the embankment to see if I could summon someone for help. I am small in stature, but I was waving my arms like a tall crazy person! An older gentlemen, who had been driving ahead of me on the road, stopped. He explained that in his rear view mirror, he'd seen my car hydroplane, so he took the next exit and returned to my rescue. He connected my car to the bumper of his truck and pulled my vehicle out of the ditch. As he talked with me, he explained how surprised he was to see that I walked away unscathed and that the only damage to my car was a dented rear bumper from slamming into the embankment. The highway patrolman soon appeared to check things out. I got back into my car, thinking I didn't want to continue this trip home anymore. But I did, and as I drove, I continued to relive the moments of the morning. Tears filled my eyes as I meditated on the words of the song, which had become my prayer, ultimately blocking any harm. God spared me on purpose, for a purpose.

PURPOSEFUL REFLECTIONS

Close calls remind us that life could end at any second, but moments such as these also remind us that God keeps us protected. We have a purpose! Count each day a blessing. Go after the dreams of your heart instead of putting them off. Live on and in purpose to the best of your ability. Remember, there is only one of each of us, and only we can fulfill our individual purpose—that task gifted by God.

"There is a time for everything, and a season for every activity under the heavens." (Ecclesiastes 3:1, NIV).

"For I know the plans I have for you," declares the Lord, "plans to prosper you and not to harm you, plans to give you hope and a future." (Jeremiah 29:11, NIV).

"But I have raised you up for this very purpose, that I might show you my power and that my name might be proclaimed in all the earth." (Exodus 9:16, NIV).

"You did not choose me, but I chose you and appointed you so that you might go and bear fruit – fruit that will last – and so that whatever you ask in my name the Father will give you." (John 15:16, NIV).

Don't let fear keep you from accomplishing your purpose. After the accident, as crazy as it may sound, I feared driving in heavy rain. I would do it, but I dreaded it. I would plan my day around the weather. I used distance as an excuse. I turned down invitations due to bad weather. I missed fun events because they were *too far*. Years later—five years to be exact—I decided that I couldn't let fear control me or keep me from accomplishing what I had to do. Weather wouldn't keep me from attending events or gathering with friends anymore. I couldn't accomplish my passion, dreams, and goals from within my carport on a rainy day. It was time to face my fear. How? I forced myself. I made a conscious decision to face it. I started small. I forced myself to drive in the rain or during storms; first, a couple of blocks from my home and eventually miles. I am proud to say that I no longer fear *bad weather*. Don't get me wrong; I certainly respect the weather, but I no longer plan my life around rain that might happen during the day.

"The Lord is with me; I will not be afraid. What can mere mortals do to me?" (Psalm 118:6, NIV).

"For the Spirit God gave us does not make us timid, but gives us power, love and self-discipline." (2 Timothy 1:7, NIV).

"So don't be afraid; you are worth more than many sparrows." (Matthew 10:31, NIV).

"So do not fear, for I am with you; do not be dismayed, for I am your God. I will strengthen you and help you; I will uphold you with my righteous right hand." (Isaiah 41:10, NIV).

"Let us not become weary in doing good, for at the

proper time we will reap a harvest if we do not give up." (Galatians 6:9, NIV).

Although we may not understand a situation or a directive from God, He wants us to go! Follow it! Do it! "By faith Abraham, when called to go to a place he would later receive as his inheritance, obeyed and went, even though he did not know where he was going" (Hebrews 11:8, NIV). In this case, Abraham witnessed his future place before he knew it was his. His visit to this place was no accident. It was ordained. You, too, may be witnessing, experiencing, or visiting places that will become your future *inheritance*.

Purpose is the reason you journey. Passion is the
fire that lights your way.

~ Author Unknown[ix]

Vann Mizzelle Lassiter

CHAPTER 3

Speak Purposefully

While growing up in a small rural community known mostly for farming peanuts, cotton, soybeans, and watermelons, it was my dream to *make something of myself* and *live beyond the county lines,* as my mom, dad, grandma, and granddad always said I would. However, it's amazing how the words of one person can change the hopes of a young, skinny, fair-skinned, curly-haired country boy with a high-pitched voice. Needless to say, the children's nursery rhyme I repeated to myself growing up whenever I faced obstacles in elementary school couldn't be further from the truth: "Sticks and stones will break my bones, but words will never hurt me."

Imagine, it's your senior year in high school and you're in the midst of one of those life-changing moments—the selecting of colleges and universities, applying for scholarships, and answering that all-important question, "Who do I want to be when I grow up?" As a student who believed in the goodness of others and certainly educators, I quickly learned the impact words could have on how I perceived my abilities and myself.

A teacher—someone hired to empower, encourage, and inspire—told me I would never make it at the state universities where I applied. She explained, "You won't be able to survive because you are too shy, quiet, and students at that school are extremely intelligent." She went on to explain that I was from a small town, had no experience living in a metropolitan-type city, and would be "homesick and back home before too long." Imagine the self-esteem level of a seventeen-year-old after hearing those words. I said nothing. I was shocked. I remembered the words of something I read in English class by Henry David Thoreau: "Go confidently in the direction of your dreams. Live the life you have imagined."[x] For me, this meant I should not be afraid to step out, have dreams, visions, hopes, and believe in miracles. Going against what I was told, I applied. I soon found that, though the battle of selecting a school was over, the battle of my mind was not.

I struggled not with grades, peer pressure, studying, roommates, or the likes, but against those words spoken into my life by an educator. I constantly asked myself, *Am I good enough? Why would someone say that if I were? Am I supposed to be here?* I stressed, literally and physically, over the words spoken by one teacher. On several occasions, I thought about transferring to a school closer to home. But my purpose was set. My destiny was pre-determined. I felt strongly that I was meant to be at that school, at that time. I remember praying one day, and God put in my spirit the message, *Don't be apologetic or feel guilty for the blessings and favor bestowed upon you. You are here for a purpose, on purpose.* As I meditated on that statement, God reminded me that He had ordered my every step. The scholarship, which allowed me to attend school, was one I had only learned about three weeks before the due date. I applied. I received it. The required test scores needed, I received right before the cutoff. One of my saving graces during this time was the assignment of a mentor, part of my scholarship program. I did not know at the time that she was from my area of the state and would serve to encourage me not to transfer or give up on my dreams. My mentor, I believe, was God-ordained. He also provided for my much needed spiritual growth. Once on campus I connected with a campus ministry through the older sister of one of my high school classmates.

This reflection revealed the awesomeness of God and His ability to weave together the fabric of our lives, designed individually yet purposefully. Seeing my life this way gave me a reason to celebrate, regardless of what others said. After I graduated with highest honor, it was interesting to see the reaction of the teacher who had been so discouraging. "I always knew you would make it," she exclaimed as if she had never said anything to the contrary. At first I thought, *really?* But then I realized I did it and overcame the mental battle despite her crippling words.

Words have power. They have the power to build one up or tear one down, encourage or discourage. Words are an integral part of purpose. Speak life. And, if by chance, words of negativity are spoken, ask God to help combat them. If need be, encourage yourself and speak positively aloud over yourself. We may not always be able to prevent the negative, dodge the obstacles, or bypass the challenges of life. But we can decide not to allow these things to affect our spirit, hinder our joy, or stop us from moving forward. Be selective about what's given time and attention, including the words you listen to. Speak on purpose and with purpose!

PURPOSEFUL REFLECTIONS

Words have assignments. Once spoken, they're on a mission to accomplish that which is predicted whether it is positive or negative. The choice to believe in their prediction, however, is ours. Be careful what's said, how it's said, and to whom it's said. Likewise, be careful what you accept from others. Remember, we do not have to hold tightly to every word that is thrown our way. No one can offend us without our permission. They can say whatever they want, but we have the right to ignore it. Choose today to overlook the negative and embrace the positive. Mentally entertain only that which builds up, encourages, motivates, inspires, and uplifts.

"Gracious words are a honeycomb, sweet to the soul and healing to the bones." (Proverbs 16:24, NIV).

"Anxiety weighs down the heart, but a kind word cheers it up." (Proverbs 12:25, NIV).

"Do not let any unwholesome talk come out of your mouths, but only what is helpful for building others up according to their needs, that it may benefit those who listen." (Ephesians 4:29, NIV).

"Those who guard their mouths and their tongues keep themselves from calamity." (Proverbs 21:23, NIV).

Things happen. All we can do is accept the circumstances, learn from them, and move forward.

We don't want to continuously place guilt or shame or harbor unforgiveness, but instead we should use everything that happens in our lives as teaching and learning tools. Use them as building blocks for strength, courage, and determination.

Forgiving those that did us wrong, talked about us, or treated us unfairly is essential. Forgiveness is just as much for us as it is for the other. As much as I would have liked not to ever speak to that teacher again, I did. I still do. As much as I would like not to like her, I am commanded to love her. I did. I do now. I had to determine that my joy, excitement for life, and destiny of my future couldn't and wouldn't be hindered or halted due to unforgiveness, regret, or sadness from one individual. My greatness is not contingent upon the words of one person, particularly not someone who lacks knowledge of my purpose or understanding of my talents. My greatness is contingent upon the many words of God.

"Brothers and sisters, I do not consider myself yet to have taken hold of it. But one thing I do: Forgetting what is behind and straining toward what is ahead, I press on toward the goal to win the prize for which God has called me heavenward in Christ Jesus." (Philippians 3:13-14, NIV).

"Bless those who persecute you; bless and do not curse." (Romans 12:14, NIV).

"Get rid of all bitterness, rage and anger, brawling and slander, along with every form of malice. Be

kind and compassionate to one another, forgiving each other, just as in Christ God forgave you." (Ephesians 4:31-32, NIV).

"Do not judge, and you will not be judged. Do not condemn, and you will not be condemned. Forgive, and you will be forgiven." (Luke 6:37, NIV)

"Your pain is the breaking of the shell that encloses your understanding."

~ Khalil Gibran[xi]

Vann Mizzelle Lassiter

CHAPTER 4

Purpose in Pain

Pain can take on several meanings. It can be physical or emotional. It might include suffering or discomfort caused by injury, distress, someone, or something. Pain can be the result of careful effort taken in completing a task. Regardless of the definition or cause, we have all endured pain to some degree. It may have been the sadness experienced after an argument with a loved one, friend, or significant other; the heartache felt after a death; the financial stress from the loss of a job and mounting bills; or physical pain due to an illness or injury. No matter the circumstance, it's uncomfortable, and it hurts. Although many would describe pain in a negative manner, it too has purpose in our lives—positive purpose.

James, the brother of Jesus and an early leader in the Church said, "Consider it pure joy, my brothers and sisters, whenever you face trials of many kinds, because you know that the testing of your faith produces perseverance. Let perseverance finish its work so that you may be mature and complete, not lacking anything." (James 1:2-4 NIV) Notice several things mentioned here. First, James tells us we should consider it *pure joy* when we face trials. This speaks of our attitude toward painful situations. Next, he tells us how these same trials are what leads us to become mature, complete, and lacking nothing. In other words, our attitude helps determine if we look at the pain in our lives as obstacles or opportunities for growth. As human beings, we all face trials or pain, and this connects us, but our response to the trial or pain is what makes us unique.

There is power in pain. How so? First, pain has the potential to protect and correct us. It tells us when something is wrong. I remember touching a hot stove as a child. I only made this mistake once because of the discomfort I felt. The nervous system within our bodies triggers a sensation that stops us from doing what might cause severe injury and lets us know that something may be wrong. When I touched the stove, an immediate message was sent from the nerves in my fingers to my brain warning me of danger. This warning resulted in an uncomfortable feeling that we refer to as *pain*. Being bothered causes one to take note and do something different (changing our thoughts and actions). In "The Surprising Purpose of Pain," Joel Runyon states, ". . . Good pain makes you stronger. Bad pain makes you smarter."[xii] When I touched the hot stove, the bad pain taught me the importance of keeping away and the only item belonging on the store was my mom's cooking pot. This painful experience made me wiser.

Pain also unifies and produces closer relationships. I remember a time when I faced a difficult situation, a time when I knew only God could fix me, save me, or bring me out. My prayer life increased exponentially. Pain brought me closer to God and strengthened my relationship with Him. I Corinthians 12:26 tells us, "If one part suffers, every part suffers with it; if one part is honored, every part rejoices with it." (NIV). In other words, as human beings, we are connected on some level. First, we are all not without suffering and joy in our lives and secondly, the suffering or joy of another could have an impact on us.

When in a painful situation, examine the root or cause of the pain then think about the lessons that can be learned from the experience. The emotional impact pain has on our lives is great, but the purpose, the lessons from the pain, is greater.

PURPOSEFUL REFLECTIONS

Scripture says, "Dear friends, do not be surprised at the fiery ordeal that has come on you to test you, as though something strange were happening to you. But rejoice inasmuch as you participate in the sufferings in Christ, so that you may be overjoyed when his glory is revealed" (1 Peter 4:12-13, NIV). Isaiah 54:17 states, "No weapon forged against you will prevail, and you will refute every tongue that accuses you" (NIV). The Lord clearly explains in these two verses that *fiery ordeals, tests,* and *weapons forged against* [us] will come, but these will be things we can handle with God's help. We will prevail over them.

God has equipped us with the strength, knowledge, and resources needed to endure the ordeals or pass the test. And, after succeeding, we will be rewarded with joy, peace, contentment, favor, and blessings. Meditate on the following quotes and scriptures during moments of pain. In the birthing of finding our way in life we may endure or face hardships, but if we trust those moments to God, we'll be rewarded beyond imagination with something beautiful, unique, and ours—purpose.

"I consider that our present sufferings are not worth comparing with the glory that will be revealed in us." (Romans 8:18, NIV).

"Success is determined not by whether or not you face obstacles, but by your reaction to them. And if you look at these obstacles as a containing fence, they become your excuse for failure. If you look at them as a hurdle, each one strengthens you for the next." (Ben Carson, *Gifted Hands: The Ben Carson Story*).[xiii]

"No one is going to hand me success. I must go out and get it myself. That's why I'm here. To dominate. To conquer. Both the world, and myself." ~ Unknown [xiv]

"He heals the brokenhearted and binds up their wounds," (Psalm 147:3, NIV).

"No temptation has overtaken you except what is common to mankind. And God is faithful; he will not let you be tempted beyond what you can bear. But when you are tempted, he will also provide a way out so that you can endure it." (I Corinthians 10:13, NIV)

Vann Mizzelle Lassiter

To accomplish great things,
we must not only act,
but also dream;
not only plan,
but also believe.

~ Anatole France[xv]

Vann Mizzelle Lassiter

CHAPTER 5

Purpose in Change

Mark Twain said, "The two most important days in your life are the day you are born and the day you find out why."[xvi] The process of finding out why God created us is a journey. This journey, like many areas of life, could very well include change, times of refocus, and redirection, ultimately leading to refinement in our knowledge of our purpose. To that end, we need not fear change, lose out in life, or slow our progression towards destiny because of fear. Instead of concentrating on our fear, we can look at change as clearer direction.

Focus encourages and feeds our souls and purpose. By placing our attention on it, we acknowledge that it's important. For example, instead of focusing on the fear of change, focus on our goals and purpose that will be accomplished because of the change. Feed your purpose—not the fear. Let's face it; change is uncomfortable. However, it is essential to growth and pushes us further into our destiny as ordained by God.

Think about the development and life cycle of the butterfly. It begins as an egg, hatches into a caterpillar, moves into the pupa stage, and finally blossoms into a beautiful butterfly. We can learn so much from this process. First, we are born, and as we grow and develop we may need to escape from things of the past, just as the caterpillar must escape from the egg.

Is there something holding you back today? What do you need to escape in order to move forward? Naysayers to your dreams? Poverty? Your current job? Hard decisions and choices may have to be made. You may need to leave some places and people behind or travel to find nourishment and maturity elsewhere. This may, in complete honesty, be unpopular, but it's essential to moving forward with God's purpose for our lives. Change, in these situations, propels us into the next level.

Frederick Douglass wrote, "If there is no struggle, there is no progress."[xvii] Just as the butterfly outgrows its egg and later its enclosed pupa stage, we sometimes outgrow people, situations, and circumstances. Embrace the growth, the change. We simply can't hold onto what used to be and also walk in the present and, ultimately, the future. As hard as change is, learn to appreciate the process. If need be, journal to record thoughts, write songs to capture feelings, paint, or find an accountability partner to discuss the process. Keep looking forward and walking towards purpose.

During the pupa stage, the caterpillar encloses itself for further development. This stage is important for the caterpillar because it allows for growth, shedding what's not needed, thereby eventually maturing into something more beautiful. Like the caterpillar, we go through stages of growth and beautification. After *shedding* our lives of negativity, development continues. Note that growth occurs in a cocoon, a shell. In other words, the change that the caterpillar undergoes to become a butterfly doesn't happen in the light, but in a dark place. Isn't it enlightening that even during dark times in our lives, we grow? Whether the darkness is the result of a conscious effort on our part to remove ourselves from a situation to think or regroup or it appears as a *gloomy* condition in our lives, we should use it as an opportunity or lesson for growth, propelling us forward in greater strength and wisdom. Finally, following the pupa stage, the butterfly appears to the world, beautiful and distinctively set apart from other insects, but yet designed on purpose with a mission.

I went through the pupa stage when I was given the opportunity to take on a new position. I am an educator with a passion and love for sharing, teaching, and learning alongside my students. The new position was out of the classroom and out of the state—the place where I was born, grew up, went to school, and taught for ten years. I was hesitant to make the move because of the connections I had with *my kids* and colleagues. Coupled with these feelings was my discomfort in change. I am a person of order, routines, and schedules. Accepting the new position meant variation, transition, and at least temporary disorder until I could establish a new routine. After a period of soul searching—looking into the job responsibilities as well as the cost of living in a new city, reading the Bible for guidance, praying, and seeking counsel from those who I knew had my best interests at heart—I made the decision to accept the new position. I took *a leap of faith.* I felt a sense of unease, but through the change I learned that my discomfort was part of my progression. Change was necessary for growth.

Looking back, I now see the new position was purposed. It provided an increase in salary, allowing me to pay off bills from college, eliminated my need to work part-time jobs, and connected me with new individuals who helped me grow personally and professionally. As I began to understand the purpose in the change, the unease was replaced with a sense of peace. Like the caterpillar emerging from the pupa stage, I emerged as a stronger person. My purpose is to encourage, inspire, and motivate others—beginning with the students in my classroom. My new position allows me to touch many more lives, and those lives will touch other lives. I'm thankful to God for this promotion—one I wasn't looking for but was granted to take me to the next level. During this transition—during this change—some colleagues didn't want me to leave and others thought I wasn't qualified for such a promotion, but God has equipped me—and you—with what is necessary for advancement.

As I reflect upon this experience of change, I am reminded of an e-mail received from a colleague, confirming the need for change in life for growth. Her e-mail read, "Heavy heart and cry, but so proud of you. God knows that (new) school could not have sought a better leader and they are so incredibly blessed to have you. Words cannot express my appreciation for you. You have helped and supported me to become a teacher not afraid to embrace change, to step outside the box, and to believe that I can do things. Be blessed, hold your head up, and do your thing. It's your season. Remember Philippians 4:13. Best wishes, M."

Do you know of someone who had to go through changes and wouldn't be where they are today without the process? Perhaps they had to make a job or career change to obtain their long awaited advancement or had to leave a bad relationship only to be freed to find true love and appreciation and a sense of value. Change is essential to one's calling, destiny, and purpose. During this time of change, remember Deuteronomy 31:6 (NIV), which states, "Be strong and courageous. Do not be afraid or terrified because of them, for the Lord your God goes with you; he will never leave you nor forsake you."

PURPOSEFUL REFLECTIONS

Don't be afraid to be set apart. It's okay to be selective in the places we visit, the friends we associate with, or the individuals with whom we share our ideas and goals. After the butterfly forges from the pupa stage, it appears as something magnificent; its colors and designs make it stand out amongst other insects. It may belong to the insect family, but its purpose and design is unique.

Ask yourself, *Am I doing what I am called to do? Am I walking in my gifting? Is my growth or development being hindered because I try to please others or fit in? Am I pleasing God?* Be authentic. One can copy the external but not the internal. Our gifts come from within. We're uniquely designed by purpose—God's purpose—and only we can execute the gifts He gave us. We must use our inward thoughts, dreams, desires, and passions to guide us purposefully into our destiny. Images fade, copies fade, counterfeits have no value; purpose is eternal and priceless.

"Before I formed you in the womb I knew you, before you were born I set you apart; I appointed you as a prophet to the nations." (Jeremiah 1:5, NIV).

"Do not be afraid of them, for I am with you and will rescue you . . ." Jeremiah 1:8 (NIV)

"Rather than viewing change as a threat and something to be feared, we will find ourselves embracing change, recognizing its potential to drive us to even higher levels of performance." (John Seely Brown, *Organizational Structures Researcher*).*xviii*

Be yourself! Many want to be the next *big thing*. Why not focus on being the next big you? We can only do this if we know who we are. Be confident in who you are and how God made you. We are, in our own right, as unique as the butterfly.

First Samuel 17:38-40 depicts part of the story of David and Goliath. Most notably, this section of scripture talks about how David could not wear the armor of someone else because it was too big. In other words, it didn't fit. He couldn't move purposefully or skillfully in the armor of Saul. Likewise, we can't wear the gifts of someone else and be successful.

"Then Saul dressed David in his own tunic. He put a coat of armor on him and a bronze helmet on his head. David fastened on his sword over the tunic and tried walking around, because he was not used to them. 'I cannot go in these,' he said to Saul, 'because I am not used to them.' So he took them off. Then he took his staff in his hand, chose five smooth stones from the stream, put them in the pouch of his shepherd's bag and, with his sling in his hand, approached the Philistine." (I Samuel 17:38-40, NIV).

"Am I now trying to win the approval of human beings, or of God? Or am I trying to please people? If I were still trying to please people, I would not be a servant of Christ." (Galatians 1:10, NIV).

"A wise man adapts himself to circumstances, as water shapes itself to the vessel that contains it." (Chinese Proverb).[xix]

"A man's gift maketh room for him, and bringeth him before great men." (Proverbs 18:16, KJV)

"What you have done is nothing compared to what you can do." (Grant Cardone)[xx]

"What the caterpillar calls the end of the world, the master calls a butterfly."

~ Richard Bach[xxi]

Vann Mizzelle Lassiter

CONCLUSION

Take a moment and think about your life—your journey. What comes to mind? Now, ask yourself, have I been walking in my calling? Am I using my gifts and talents? Am I happy? Fulfilled?

Remember, purpose includes a decision. Like salvation, God has given purpose to us for free, but it is up to us to walk in it and work in it. God, who Himself is purpose, created us.

As we seek to live a purposeful life—a fulfilling life—remember that we were born purposed. No human gave it to us.

How will you live in and on purpose today and in the days to come?

Vann Mizzelle Lassiter

"Do not go where the path may lead, go instead
where there is no path and leave a trail."

~ Ralph Waldo Emerson[xxii]

.

ABOUT THE AUTHOR

Vann Mizzelle Lassiter—educator, motivational speaker, and author—is known for his exuberant outlook on life and energetic demeanor. Though raised in a small rural town in northeastern North Carolina, Vann has global dreams and worldwide ambitions. He is an avid traveler who believes in self-growth through life's challenges. Determined to *live in and on purpose*, his desire is to share his love for life and learning by encouraging others to use their gifts to change the world.

Vann is a graduate of North Carolina State University with a Bachelor of Science degree in Business and Marketing Education and a Masters in Education degree in Curriculum and Instruction. He attained his doctoral degree from Old Dominion University in Occupational and Technical Studies – Career and Technical Education and is the winner of several awards and recognitions including being named the 2010-2011 North Carolina AT&T Region 1 (Northeast) Regional Teacher of the Year.

Vann Mizzelle Lassiter

Endnotes

---

[i] Tubman, Harriet. Public domain.

[ii] Roosevelt, Eleanor. Public domain per National First Ladies' Library.

[iii] http://www.merriam-webster.com/dictionary/purpose. August 2015.

[iv] Babe Ruth Central, The Site That Ruth Built, Ruth's Childhood. www.baberuthcentroal.com/babe-ruth-biography/ruths-childhood/. Used by permission.

[v] Beaver, Rev. Jerry W., *Spiritual Muscle—Six Months to Building Spiritual Strength*. Copyright © 2015 by Baptist Growth. Used by permission. www.baptistgrowth.com

[vi] Anonymous African Proverb.

[vii] Lincoln, Abraham. Public Domain.

[viii] Norful, Smokie. *I Need You Now.* 2003. Used by permission.

[ix] Author Unknown

[x] Thoreau, Henry David. Public Domain

[xi] Gibran, Khalil. *The Prophet.* Alfred A Knopf. 1923.

[xii] Runyon, Joel. *The Surprising Purpose of Pain.* Impossible. http://impossiblehq.com/surprising-purpose-pain/ August 2015. Used by permission.

[xiii] Carson, Ben. Gifted Hands: The Ben Carson Story. Zondervan. December 8, 1996. Used by permission.

[xiv] Author Unknown

[xv] France, Anatole. Public Domain

[xvi] Twain, Mark. Public Domain.

[xvii] Douglas, Frederick. An address on West India Emancipation – Aug. 3, 1857. Public Domain.

[xviii] Brown, John Seely. *Organizational Structures Researcher.*
http://georgecouros.ca/blog/archives/3890. August 2015.

[xix] Chinese Proverb. www.quotes.net. August 2015.

[xx] Cardone, Grant. May 4, 2015.
http://twitter.com/grantcardone/status/595241278855589888

[xxi] Bach, Richard. Illusions: The Adventures of a Reluctant Messiah. Heinemann; 19th printing edition. 1977.

[xxii] Emerson, Ralph Waldo. Public Domain

www.ingramcontent.com/pod-product-compliance
Lightning Source LLC
Chambersburg PA
CBHW071852020426
42331CB00007B/1970